FIDDLE TUNES
FOR
Baritone Ukulele
BY DICK SHERIDAN

To access audio visit:
www.halleonard.com/mylibrary
Enter Code
2963-1965-6734-4081

ISBN 978-1-57424-323-9
SAN 683-8022

UKULELES

Baritone Ukulele
BK-35

All-Solid Mahogany

Cover by James Creative Group

Contents

About The Arranger

Dick Sheridan admits he does not play the fiddle. He's tried, but being far-sighted he could never focus on the close-up fingering required for the instrument. Attempts only brought squinty headaches and howls of protest from the family cat, bringing to mind the old chant "I had a cat and her name was Daisy, and when I played the cat went crazy!"

Being unable to play the fiddle did not diminish his love for fiddle tunes. A few he could play on the guitar, some others on the tenor and 5-string banjos, but never with the ease and satisfaction that these lively tunes demanded. What a pleasant discovery to find that they could be played so readily on the ukulele, specifically the baritone whose tuning allowed the wide range of many fiddle tunes. And how much easier to keep close at hand the small, lightweight ukulele rather than one of the larger instruments with their limitations of size and playability.

Dick found that plowing through fiddle tune books, manuscripts, sheet music, and instructional methods required a high level of skill in reading standard notation. Converting to tablature made playing much easier, while adding chords enriched the playing experience by combining harmony with the melody.

Selecting tunes for this book proved challenging. There are literally hundreds, if not thousands, of tunes to draw from. As Dick culled through the literature and sound archives, one by one a roster of favorites gradually took shape. What follows is a definitive collection of prime choices.

The melodies of these tunes are truly enjoyable. They provide an excellent diversion for occasionally digressing from the ukulele's usual repertoire. Some tunes are easy, others more demanding, but all are delightful and worth the effort of being explored.

Dick looks forward to sharing with you each and every tune. He feels sure you'll agree that once again the ukulele justifies its popularity by adding yet another dimension to its already broad versatility.

~*~

Introduction

The versatile uke. How true the saying that good things come in small packages. The uke may be diminutive in size but it's certainly enormous in potential. Just look for example at the wide range of exciting titles offered in Centerstream's extensive catalog of great books for the ukulele. You'll find a vast wealth of topics --gospel music and classics, nautical ballads and Stephen Foster treasures, vintage numbers from World War I, college alma maters, cowboy and Hawaiian songs, Gilbert and Sullivan favorites, ethnic music, folk songs, and selections for the holidays.

Now comes fiddle tunes for the ukulele! And why not? The uke can handle it all, the spirited melodies and the full assortment of chords to match. There's no reason why fiddle tunes should be limited to just the fiddle.

Although it's impossible for the uke's gentle voice to rival the volume of a fiddle, say at a square dance or hoedown, that doesn't diminish its capability for great sound in more limited surroundings.

You may wonder why this collection was arranged for the baritone ukulele instead of its smaller relations, the soprano, concert, and tenor. The answer is a matter of range. The expansive range of fiddle tunes doesn't always fit the tuning of the smaller ukes. However that doesn't prevent these smaller ukes from joining in on the fun. They certainly can play some of the melodies, and by adding back-up chords their higher pitch will lend a special ingredient to the mix.

Even with the wide range of the baritone, occasionally sections of the melodies need to be dropped or raised an octave if they require extremely high or low frets. Standard keys that fit the fiddle sometimes need to be transposed for the uke, but the sense of the tune is never compromised.

The domain of the fiddle these days is primarily that of bluegrass, country/western, and old-time string band events, with a fair amount of Irish, Cajun and British Isles performances thrown in. Square dancing is still popular, but not to the degree that it once was. Every small town used to have its Saturday night barn dance with a band composed of local amateur musicians. It's amusing to note how those musicians often adopted the persona of rural rubes or mountain hillbillies. They sported chin whiskers, blacked-out teeth, overalls, and hats fancied to be like those worn by moonshining mountaineers. Thankfully, there's no need for ukulele players to affect a similar image.

Dance music was arranged in sets, usually four or five tunes per set, and perhaps that's something to be considered for uke players. The tunes performed were mostly ones found in this book, plus a few popular songs of the day. Here's a typical set:

Arkansas Traveler
Turkey in the Straw
Miss McLeod's Reel
Soldier's Joy
Pop Goes the Weasel

Titles of fiddle tunes are almost as intriguing as the music itself listed. Check out the Table of Contents to see the extent of imagination. Some titles are straightforward, some puzzling, but most create vivid and colorful pictures. Humor is no exception. Take for example "Napoleon Crossing His Eyes" – a Canadian variation of the tunes that have Napoleon crossing the Alps and the Rhine.

Besides learning tunes from other players, fiddlers often acquired tunes from recordings, some going back to the early days of Edison cylinders. These recordings might feature only a single song or a medley. One release from the Edison Company in 1919 is the "Devil's Dream Medley" which included "Arkansas Traveler," Devil's Dream," "Old Zip Coon" "Chicken Reel," along with others.

The CD recordings with this book are intended to introduce unfamiliar songs and to hear the arrangements and supporting harmony of the chords. Tempos are presented at reasonable speed to facilitate learning, but be prepared for triplets and fast chord changes. Finally, it's up to you as to whatever tempo is comfortable. Play at your own speed. Tunes are fun at any speed. Use a pick or play finger-style with your thumb, index, or other fingers.

In addition, many of the tunes in this book can be heard on the computer, although it must be remembered that there can be variations with the same title. A good number of fiddle tunes have their roots in folk traditions where there's much latitude in evolution.

An interesting claim of folklore is that when a fiddle is not being played and tucked away in its case, it should be wrapped in silk. That's supposed to bring good luck. Another practice is to drop a rattlesnake's rattle into the fiddle. This too supposedly brings good luck and improves the sound. Whether either of these practices is effective seems to be a matter of opinion.

What about the uke? Would silk and a snake rattle bring good fortune and better sound? Not too practical, you say. After all, it's only folklore. Or is there more to it than that? You be the judge.

With or without silk and rattles, good times are already coming your way in the form of the fabulous tunes that follow representing some of the best and most popular numbers played by fiddlers past and present. Whether for the fiddle or uke, these tunes are a musical treasury, time proven and enduring, a legacy for music makers that spans generations and continents.

Let the fiddlers rosin their bows and strike up a merry tune. But now their tunes are no longer solely their own. With picking and strumming uke players are able to share the music, expand their repertoires, and join in on the fun. Exciting new material is in store in the pages that follow. Get ready for a musical adventure: it's ready and waiting, and it's all yours for the taking!

~*~

ARKANSAS TRAVELER

Baritone ukulele tuning: DGBE

TRADITIONAL

ASH GROVE

Baritone ukulele tuning: DGBE

TRADITIONAL

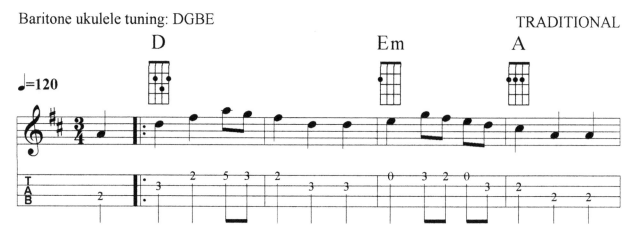

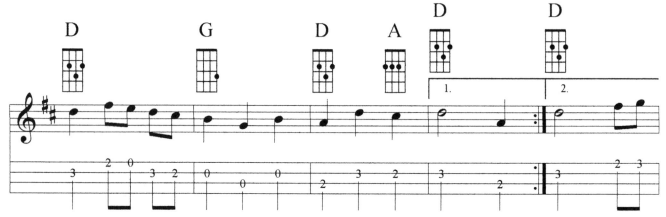

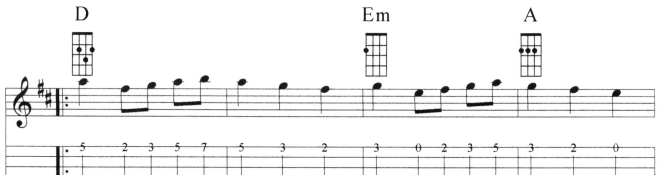

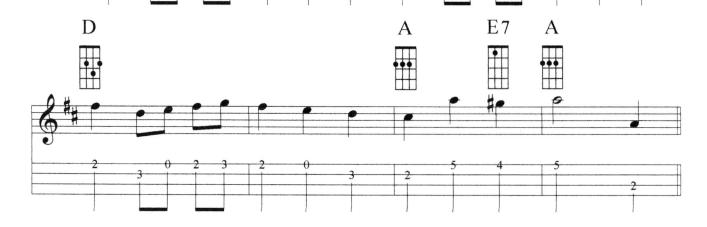

ASH GROVE

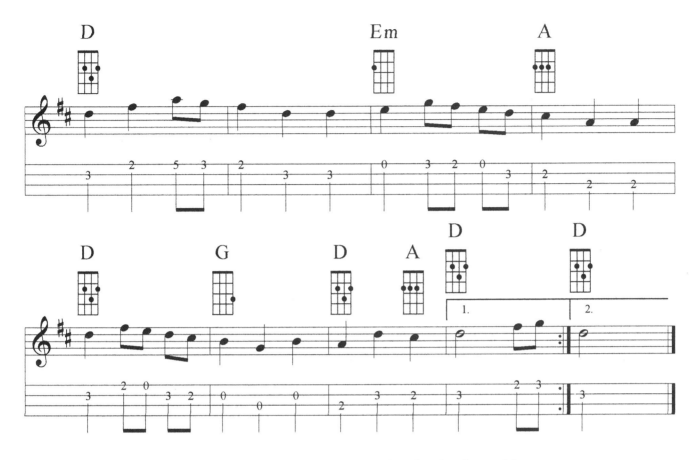

This traditional waltz from Wales can be found with other beautiful tunes
in Centerstream's publication "Celtic Songs for the Tenor Banjo."

Harold Crosby, Charles Taggatt, Dan Ross

BILLY IN THE LOWGROUND

Baritone ukulele tuning: DGBE

TRADITIONAL

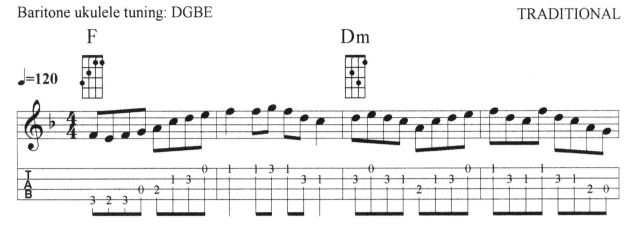

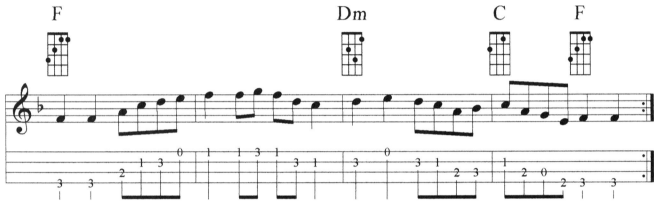

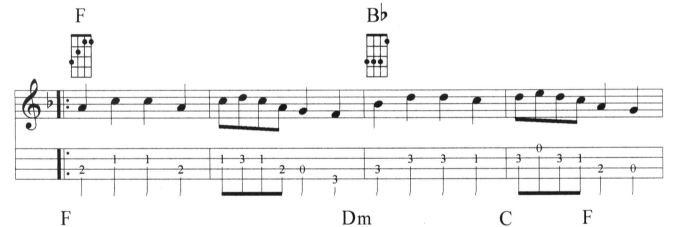

BONAPARTE'S RETREAT

Baritone ukulele tuning: DGBE

TRADITIONAL

THE BOYS OF BLUEHILL

Baritone ukulele tuning: DGBE

TRADITIONAL

THE BOYS OF BLUEHILL

BULLY OF THE TOWN

Baritone ukulele tuning: DGBE

CHARLES E. TREVATHAN

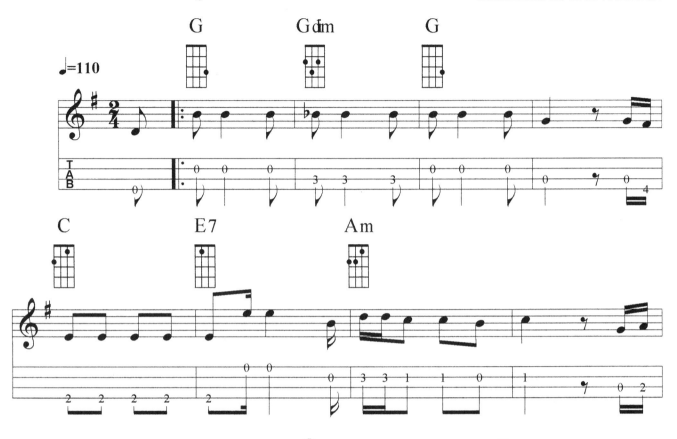

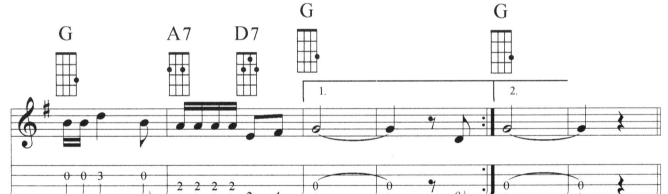

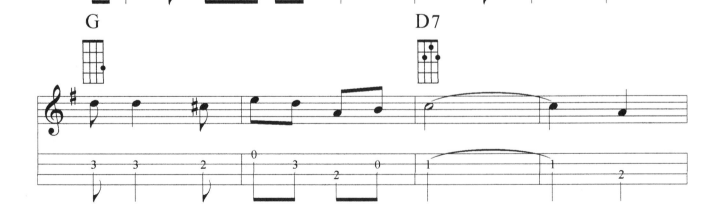

BULLY OF THE TOWN

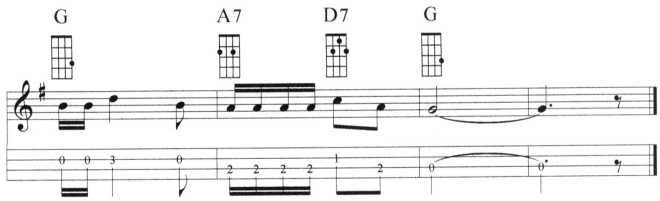

CHERISH THE LADIES

Baritone ukulele tuning: DGBE

TRADITIONAL

DURANG'S HORNPIPE

Baritone ukulele tuning: DGBE

TRADITIONAL

DEVIL'S DREAM

Baritone ukulele tuning: DGBE

TRADITIONAL

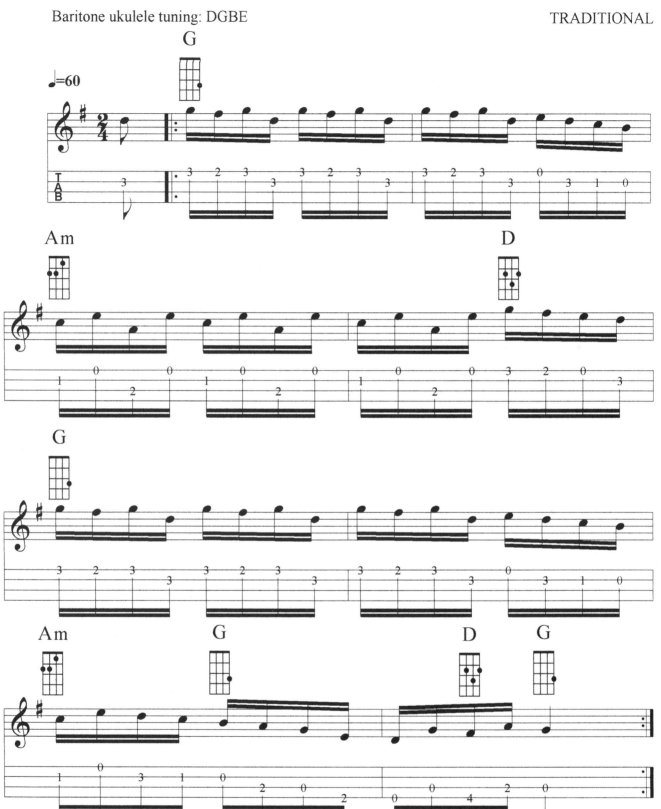

DEVIL'S DREAM

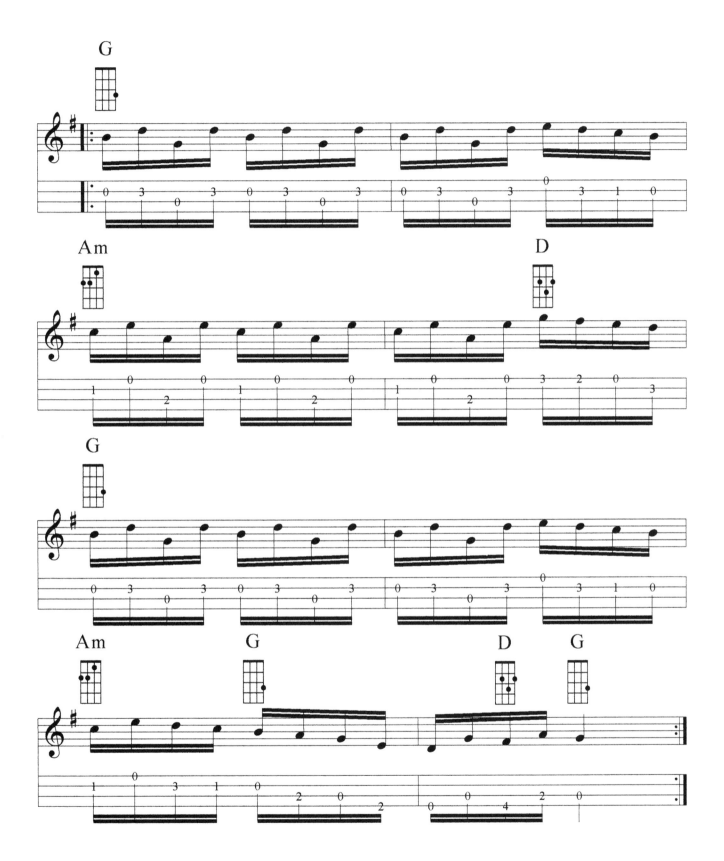

THE EIGHTH OF JANUARY
(BATTLE OF NEW ORLEANS)

Baritone ukulele tuning: DGBE

TRADITIONAL

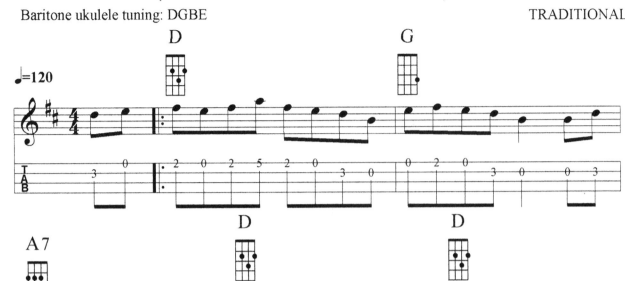

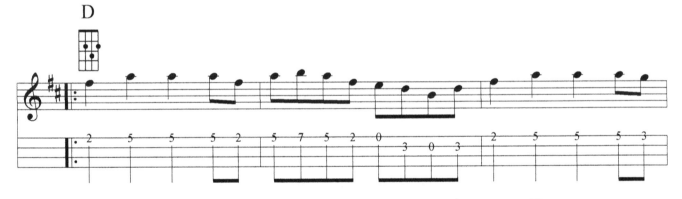

FAREWELL TO WHISKEY

Baritone ukulele tuning: DGBE

Traditional

FLOP-EARED MULE

Baritone ukulele tuning: DGBE

TRADITIONAL

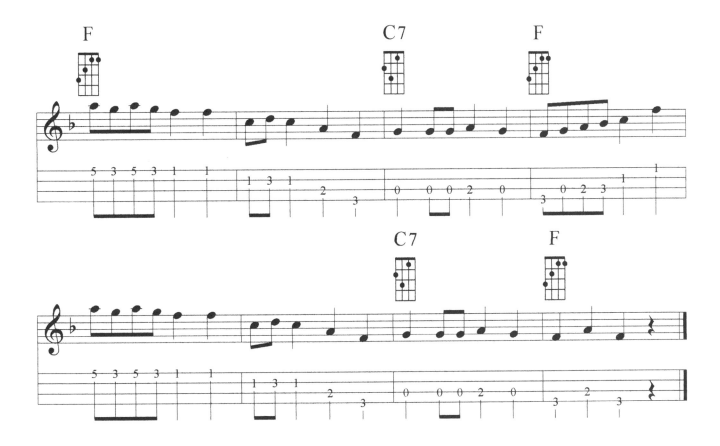

Oklahoma Night Riders

GÅNGLÅT FRÅN MOCKFJÄRD

Baritone ukulele tuning: DGBE

TRADITIONAL SCANDINAVIAN

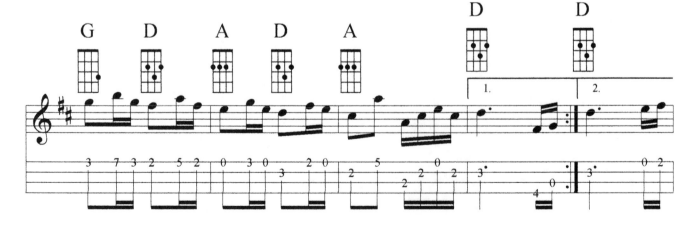

24

GÅNGLÅT FRÅN MOCKFJÄRD

GARRYOWEN

Baritone ukulele tuning: DGBE

TRADITIONAL

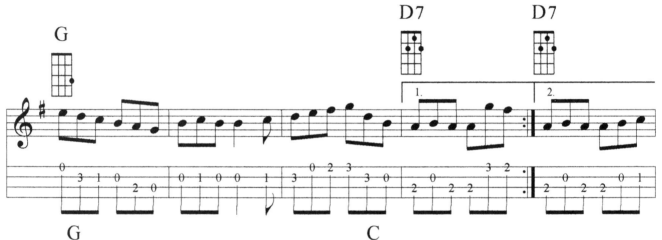

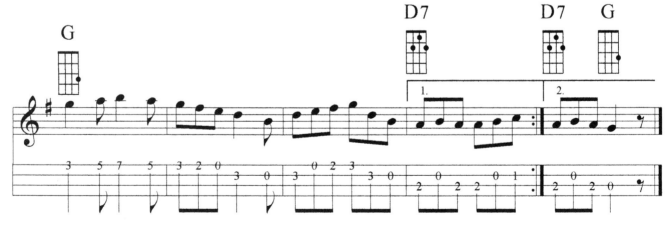

THE GIRL I LEFT BEHIND ME

Baritone ukulele tuning: DGBE

TRADITIONAL

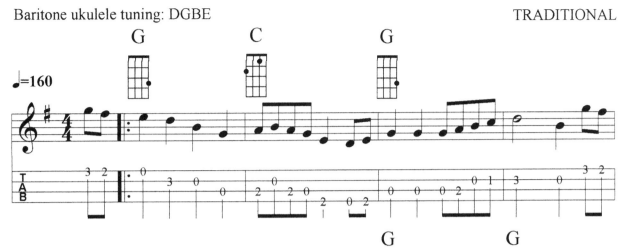

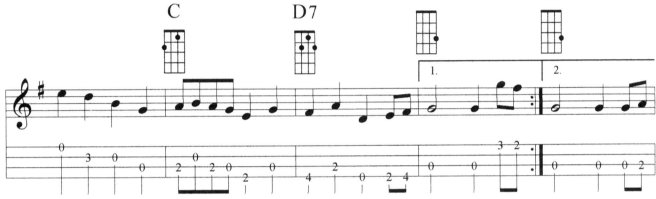

GOLDEN SLIPPERS

Baritone ukulele tuning: DGBE

TRADITIONAL

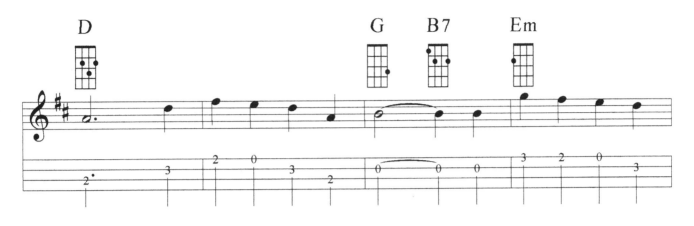

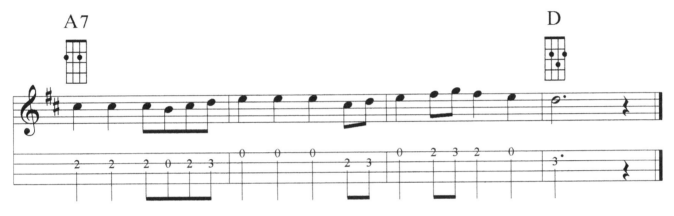

GRANDPA'S WALTZ

Baritone ukulele tuning: DGBE

TRADITIONAL

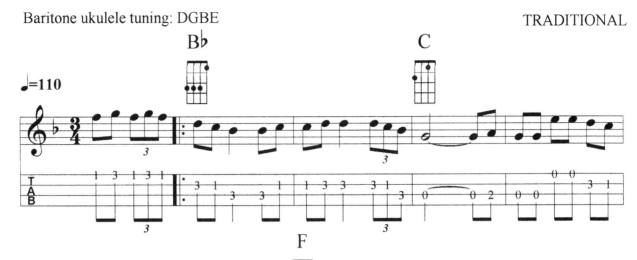

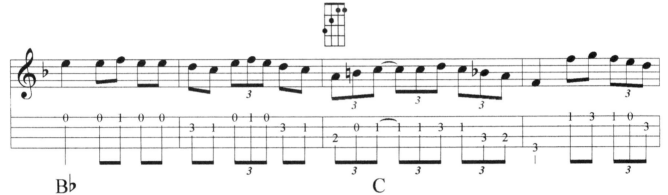

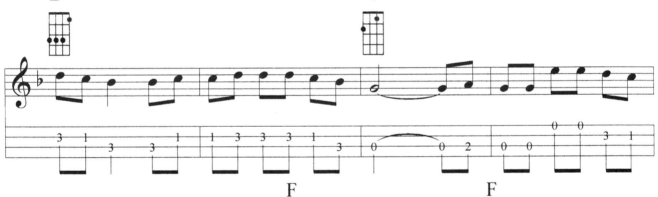

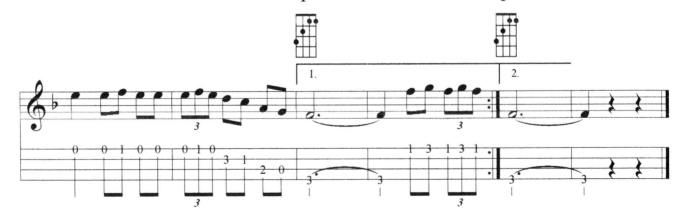

HASTE TO THE WEDDING

Baritone ukulele tuning: DGBE

TRADITIONAL

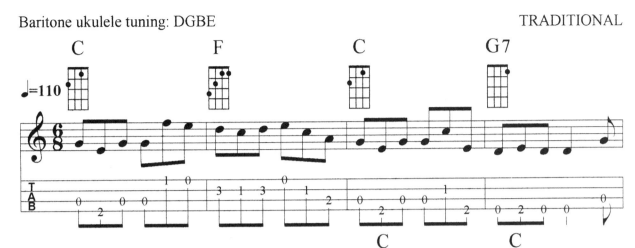

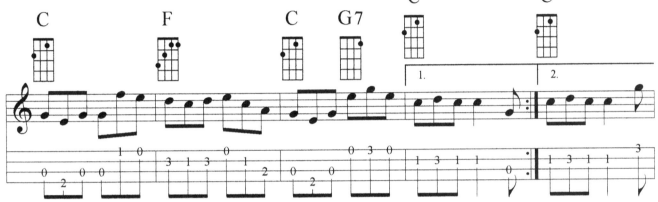

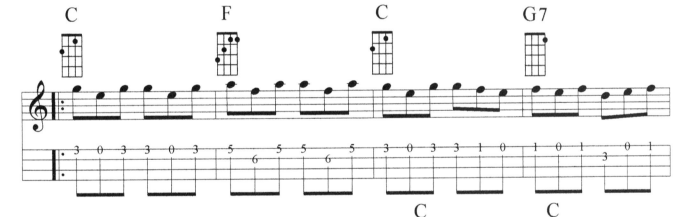

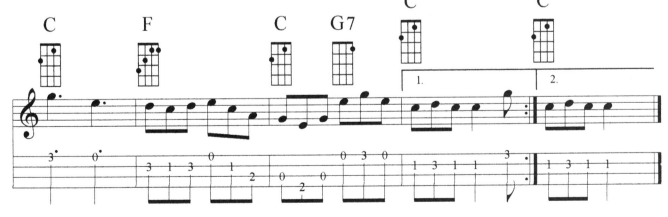

HARVEST HOME

Baritone ukulele tuning: DGBE

TRADITIONAL

HARVEST HOME

IRISH WASHERWOMAN

Baritone ukulele tuning: DGBE

TRADITIONAL

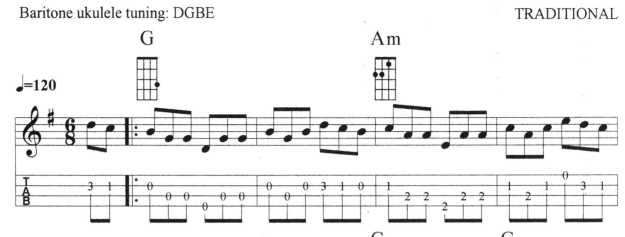

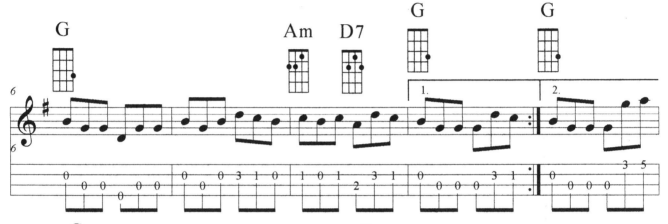

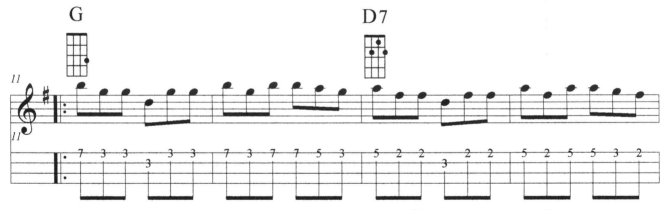

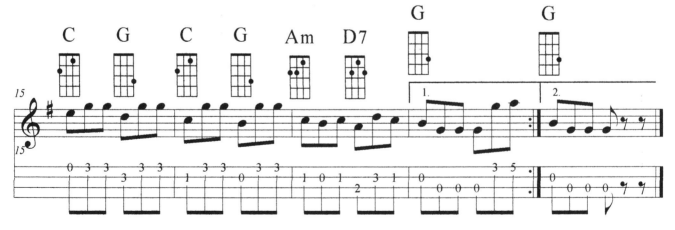

JACKY TAR

Baritone ukulele tuning: DGBE

TRADITIONAL

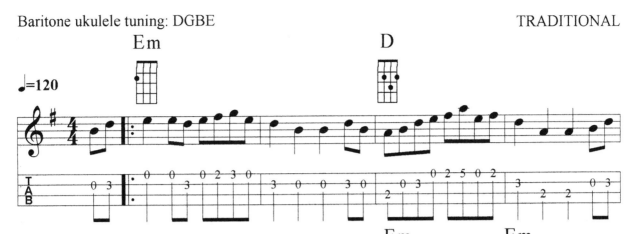

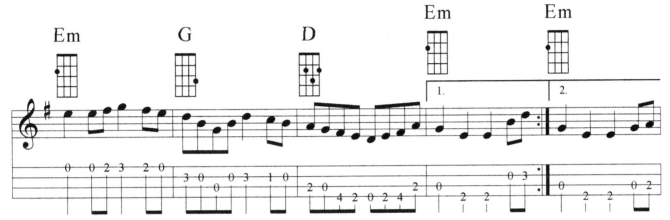

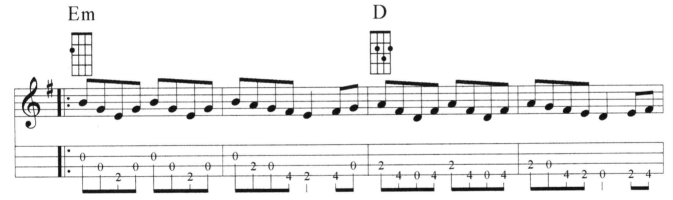

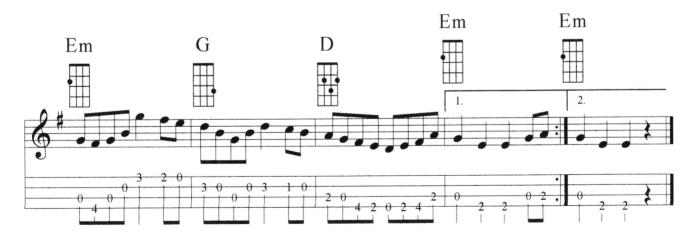

JOLIE BLONDE

(The "Cajun National Anthem")

Baritone ukulele tuning: DGBE

TRADITIONAL

LANNIGAN'S BALL

Baritone ukulele tuning: DGBE

TRADITIONAL

KING OF THE FAIRIES

Baritone ukulele tuning: DGBE

TRADITIONAL

KING OF THE FAIRIES

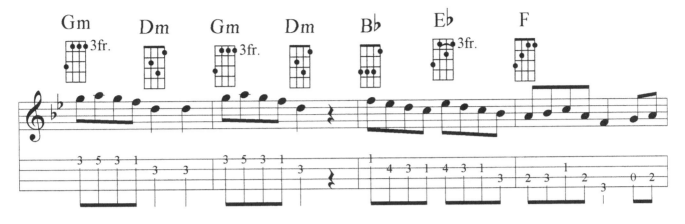

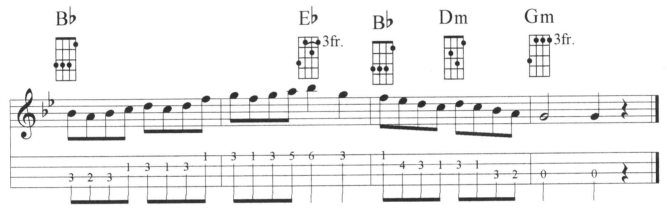

*The late great
Bill Tapia*

39

LEATHER BRITCHES

Baritone ukulele tuning: DGBE

TRADITIONAL

LIBERTY

Baritone ukulele tuning: DGBE

TRADITIONAL

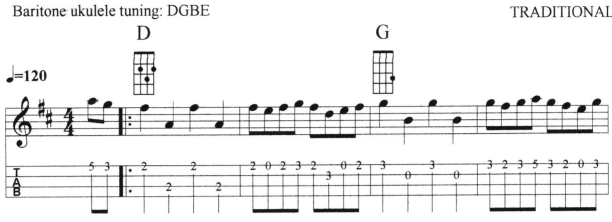

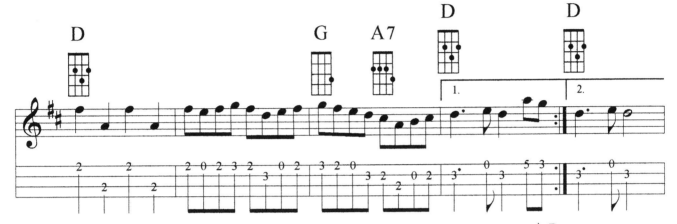

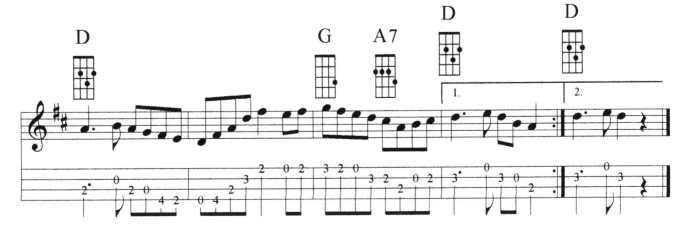

MASON'S APRON

Baritone ukulele tuning: DGBE

TRADITIONAL

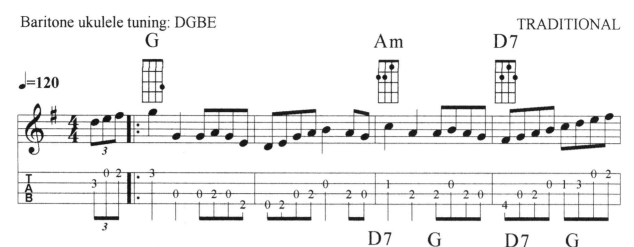

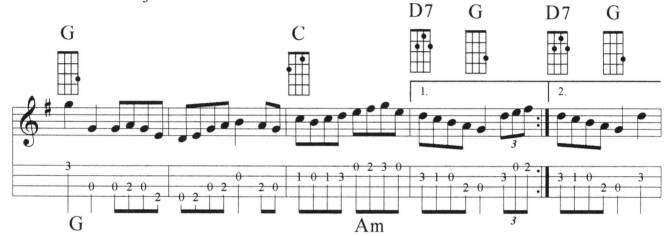

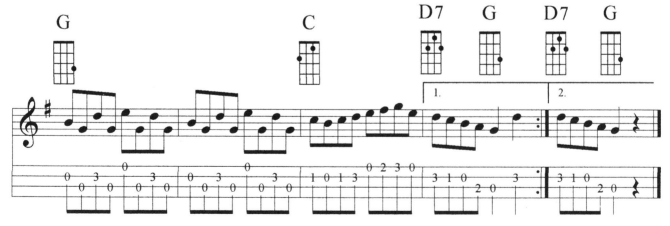

MISS McLEOD'S REEL

Baritone ukulele tuning: DGBE

TRADITIONAL

MORPETH RANT

Baritone ukulele tuning:DGBE

TRADITIONAL

MUCKIN' O' GEORDIE'S BYRE

Baritone ukulele tuning: DGBE

TRADITIONAL

♩=130

NAPOLEON CROSSING THE ALPS

Baritone ukulele tuning: DGBE

TRADITIONAL

NAPOLEON CROSSING THE ALPS

NAPOLEON CROSSING THE RHINE

Baritone ukulele tuning: DGBE

TRADITIONAL

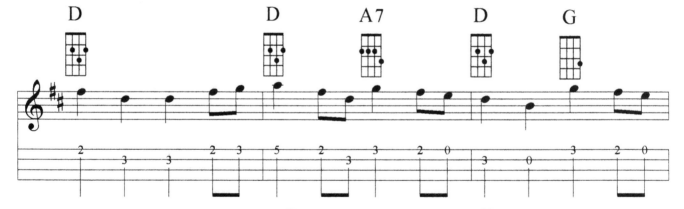

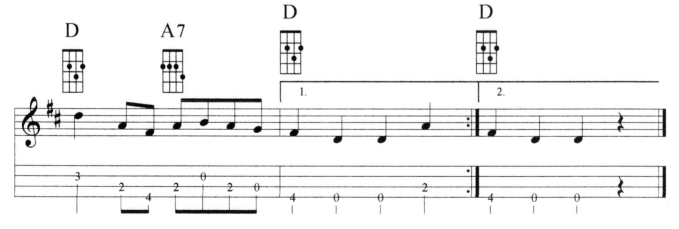

O'GALLAGHER'S FROLICS

Baritone ukulele tuning: DGBE

TRADITIONAL

OLD ROSIN, THE BEAU

Baritone ukulele tuning: gCEA

TRADITIONAL

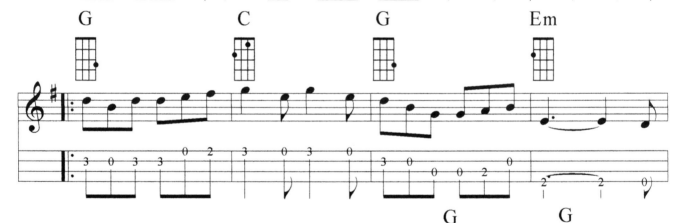

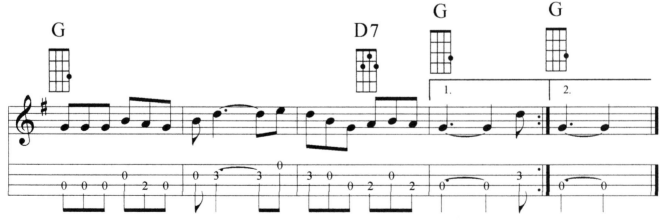

OVER THE WATER TO CHARLIE

Baritone ukulele tuning: DGBE

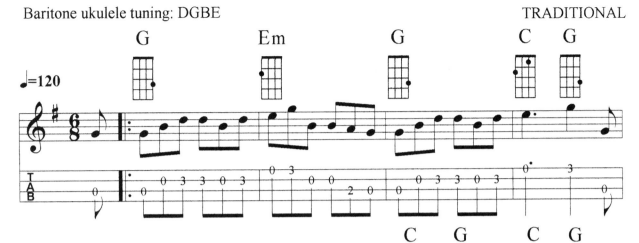

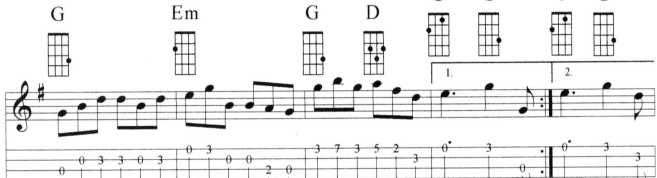

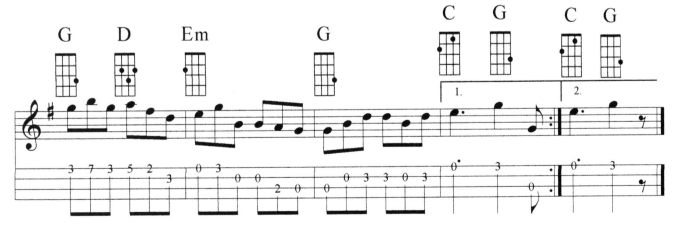

OVER THE WATERFALL

Ukulele tuning: gCEA

Traditional

PLANXTY IRWIN

Baritone ukulele tuning: DGBE

TRADITIONAL

POP GOES THE WEASEL

Baritone ukulele tuning: DGBE

TRADITIONAL

RAGTIME ANNIE

Baritone ukulele tuning: DGBE

TRADITIONAL

THE RAKES OF MALLOW

Baritone ukulele tuning DGBE

TRADITIONAL

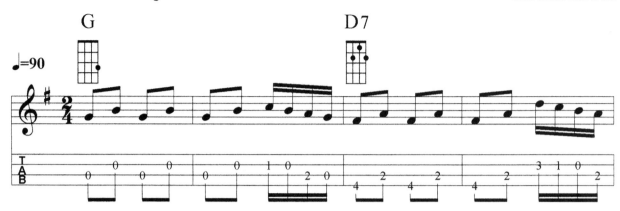

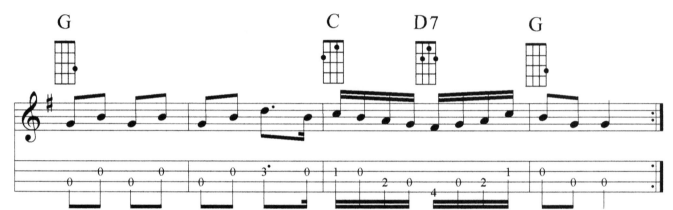

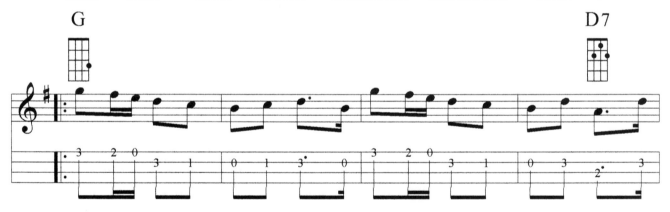

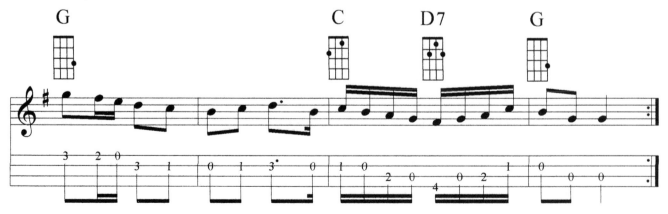

RICKETT'S HORNPIPE

Baritone ukulele tuning: DGBE

TRADITIONAL

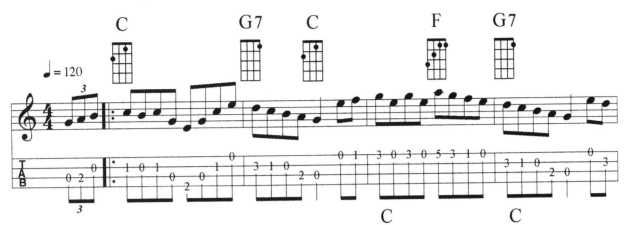

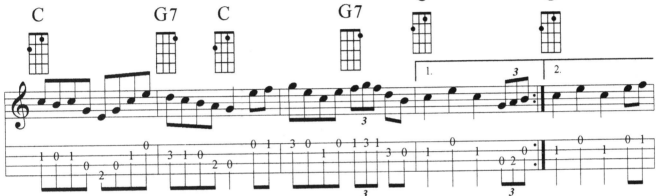

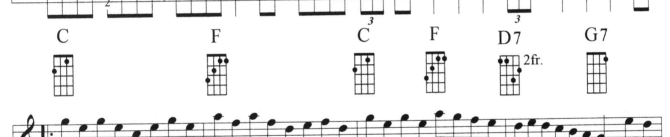

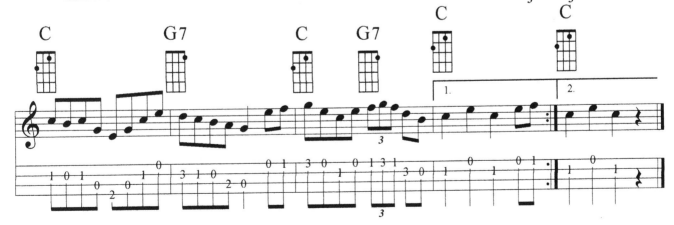

RED HAIRED BOY

Baritone ukulele tuning: DGBE

TRADITIONAL

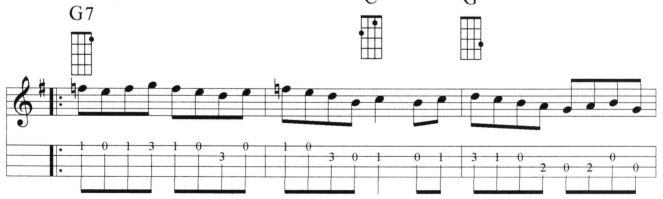

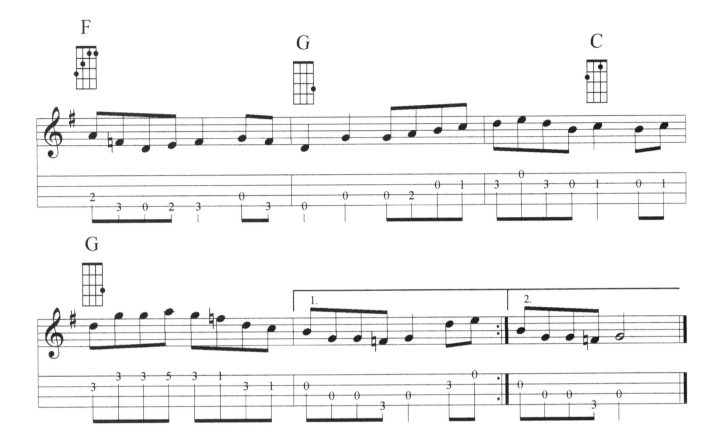

RUBER DOLLY

Baritone ukulele tuning: DGBE

TRADITIONAL

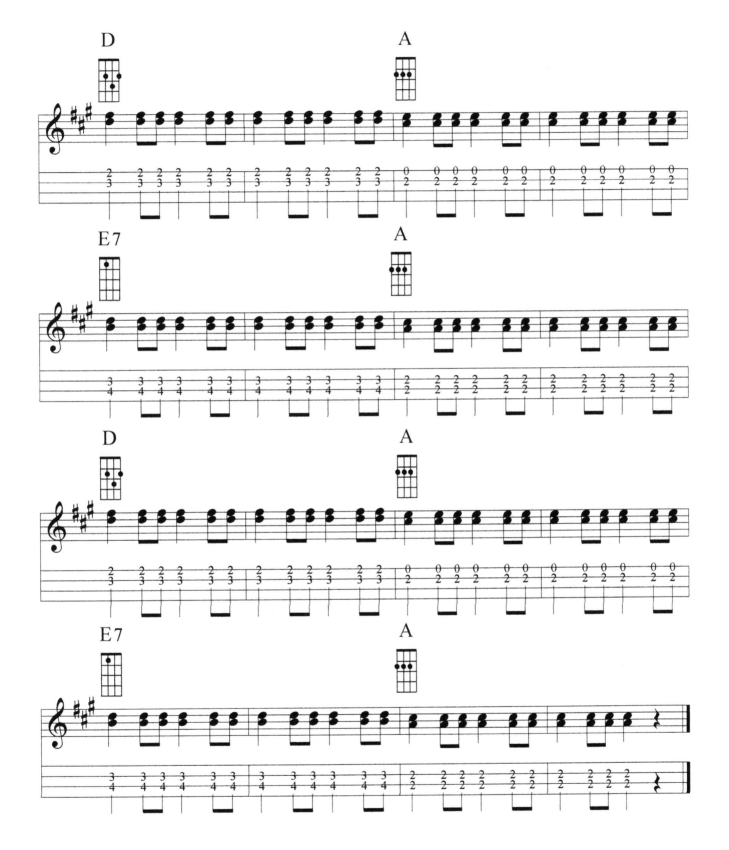

SADDLE THE PONY

Baritone ukulele tuning DGBE

TRADITIONAL

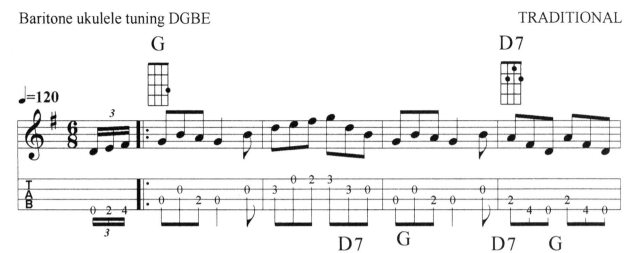

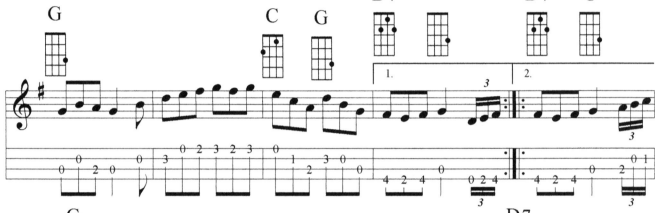

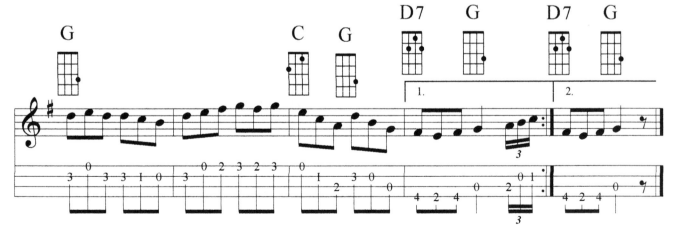

SAILOR'S HORNPIPE

Baritone ukulele tuning: DGBE

TRADITIONAL

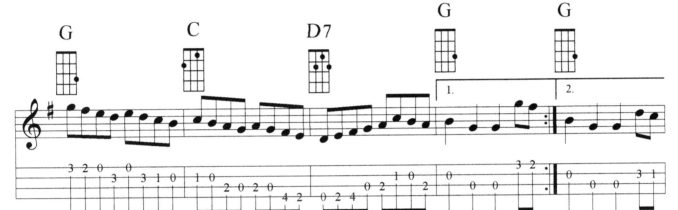

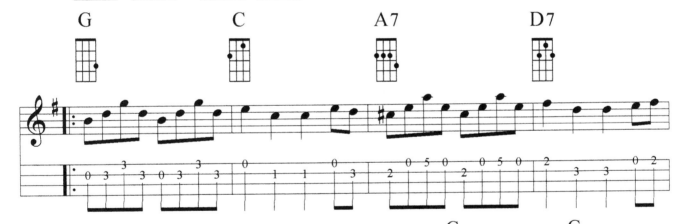

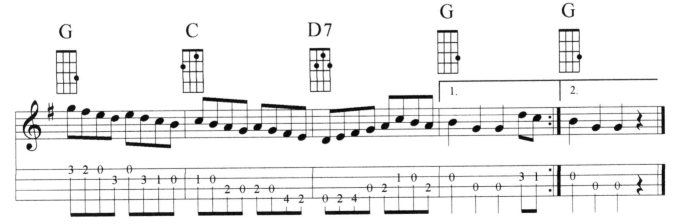

SALLY GOODIN

Baritone ukulele tuning: DGBE

TRADITIONAL

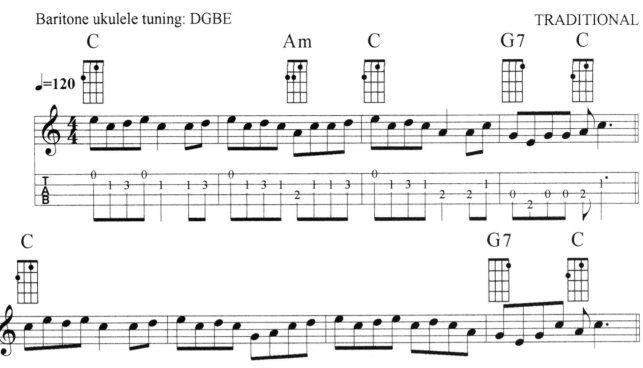

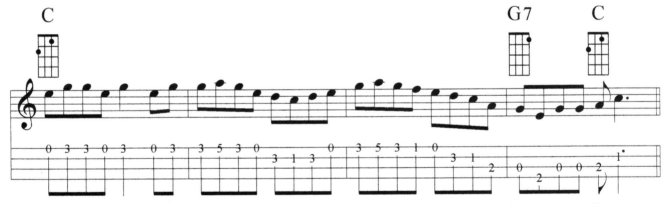

SCOTLAND THE BRAVE

Baritone ukulele tuning: DGBE

TRADITIONAL

SOLDIER'S JOY

Baritone ukulele tuning: DGBE

TRADITIONAL

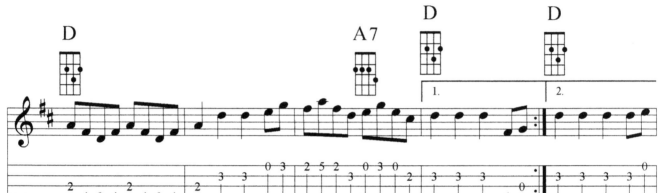

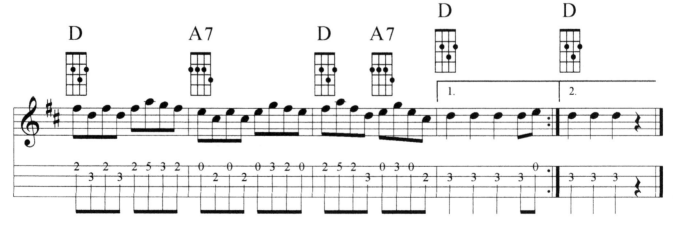

ST. ANNE'S REEL

Baritone ukulele tuning: DGBE

TRADITIONAL

STATEN ISLAND

Baritone ukulele tuning: DGBE

TRADITIONAL

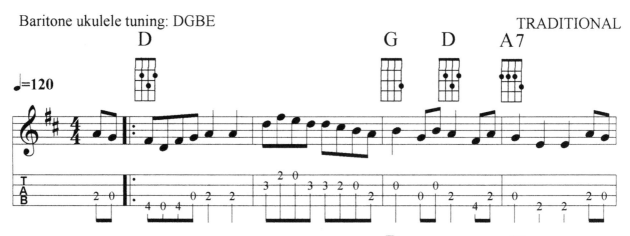

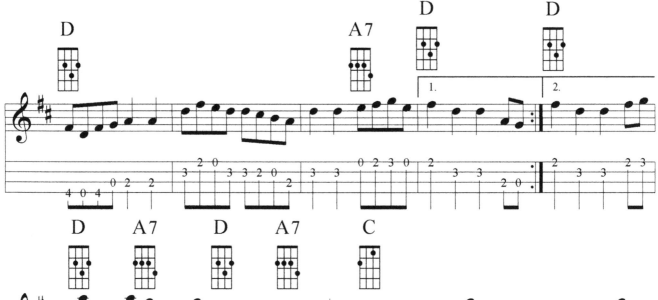

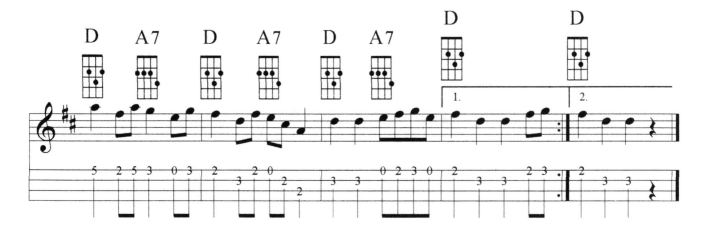

SWALLOW TAIL JIG

Baritone ukulele tuning: DGBE

TRADITIONAL

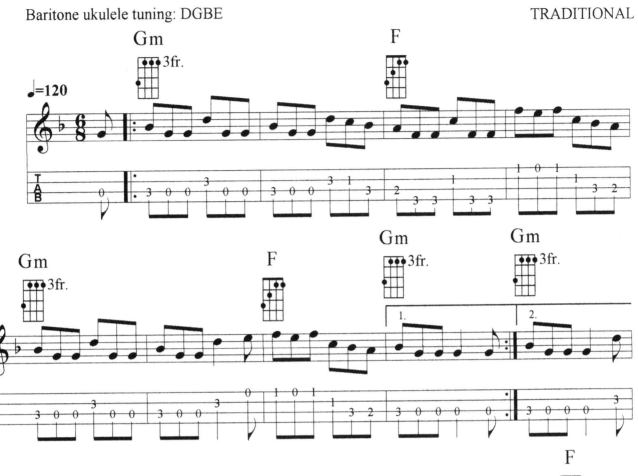

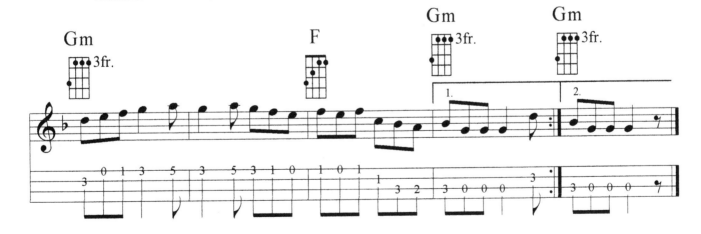

TEMPEST

Baritone ukulele tuning: DGBE

TRADITIONAL

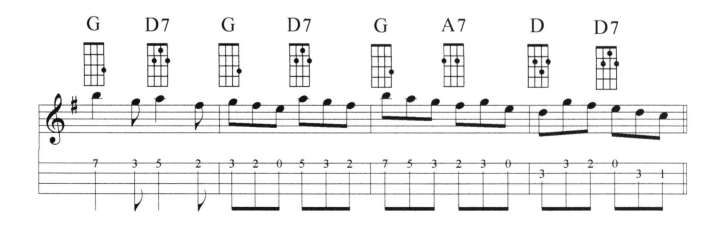

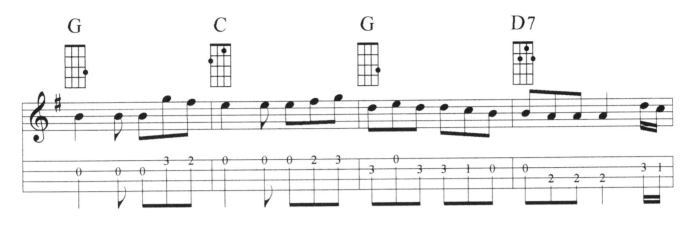

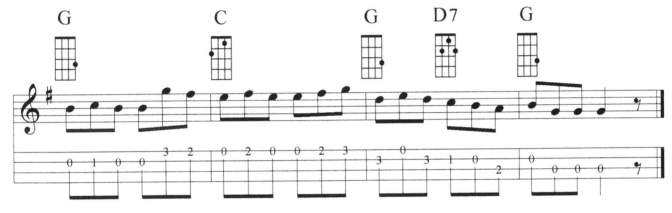

TURKEY IN THE STRAW

Baritone ukulele tuning: DGBE

TRADITIONAL

WHISKEY BEFORE BREAKFAST

Baritone ukulele tuning: DGBE

TRADITIONAL

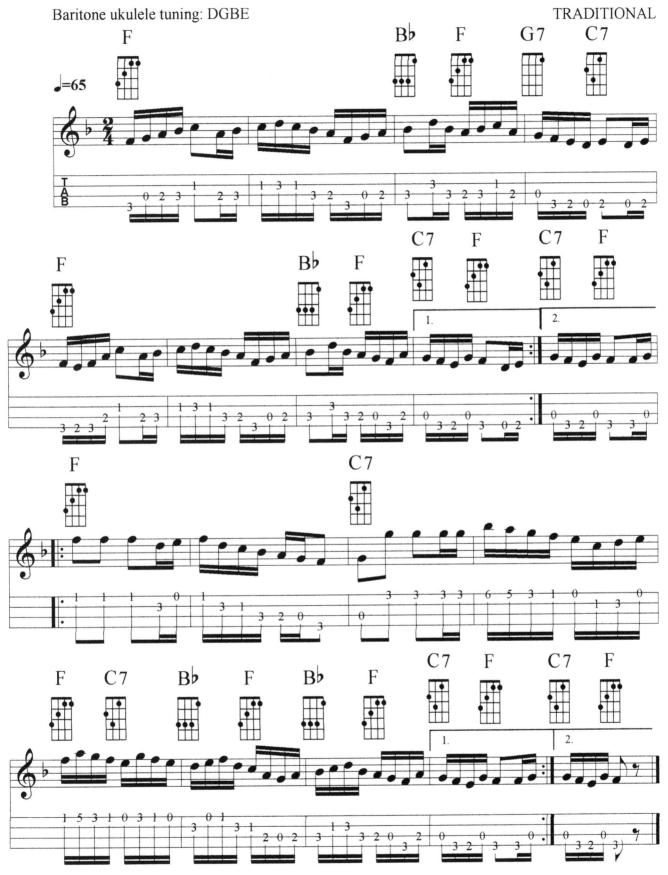

WIND THAT SHAKES THE BARLEY

Baritone ukulele tuning: DGBE

TRADITIONAL

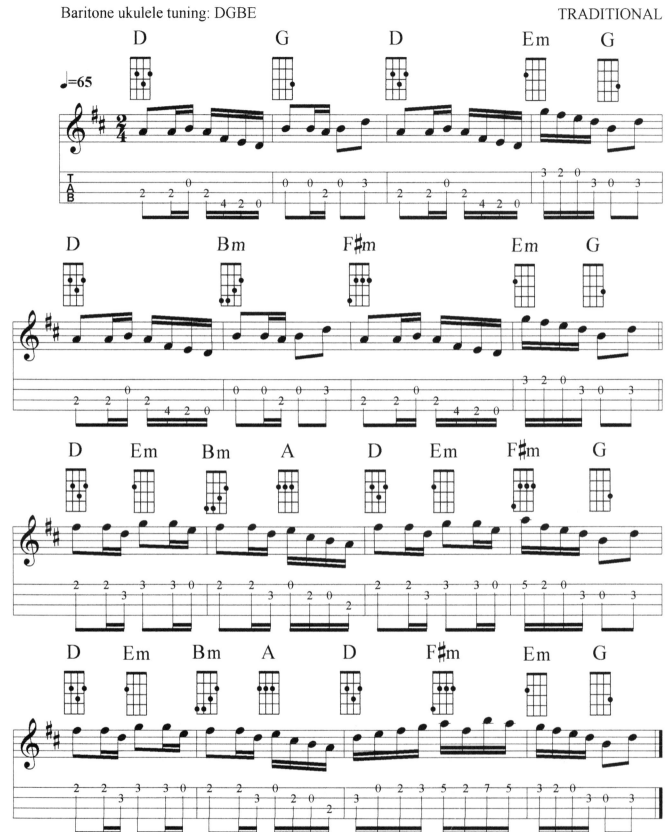

More Great Books from Dick Sheridan...

More Great Ukulele Books from Centerstream...

CHRISTMAS UKULELE, HAWAIIAN STYLE

Play your favorite Christmas songs Hawaiian style with expert uke player Chika Nagata. This book/CD pack includes 12 songs, each played 3 times: the first and third time with the melody, the second time without the melody so you can play or sing along with the rhythm-only track. Songs include: Mele Kalikimaka (Merry Christmas to You) • We Wish You a Merry Christmas • Jingle Bells (with Hawaiian lyrics) • Angels We Have Heard on High • Away in a Manger • Deck the Halls • Hark! The Herald Angels Sing • Joy to the World • O Come, All Ye Faithful • Silent Night • Up on the Housetop • We Three Kings.
00000472 Book/CD Pack $19.95

FUN SONGS FOR UKULELE
INCLUDES TAB

50 terrific songs in standard notation and tablature for beginning to advanced ukulele players. Includes Hawaiian songs, popular standards, classic Western, Stephen Foster and more, with songs such as: The Darktown Strutters Ball • I'm Always Chasing Rainbows • Hot Lips • Gentle Annie • Maikai Waipio • Whispering • Ja-Da • China Boy • Colorado Trail • and many more. Also includes a chord chart and a special section on how to hold the ukulele.
00000407...$14.95

ULTIMATE LIT'L UKULELE CHORDS, PLUS
INCLUDES TAB

by Kahuna Uke (aka Ron Middlebrook)
This handy 6' x 9' guide in the popular C tuning provides all the ukulele chords you'll ever need or use. The diagrams are easy to use and follow, with all the principal chords in major and minor keys, in all the different chords positions. Plus, there are sections on How to Begin, Scales on All Strings, Note Studies, and Chord Modulations (great to use for intros & endings!). This handy 32 page guide fits right in a case perfectly. Happy strumming, you'll Mahalo me latter.
00001351...$7.99

ASAP UKULELE
INCLUDES TAB

Learn How to Play the Ukulele Way
by Ron Middlebrook
This easy new method will teach you the ukulele ASAP! Each exercise in the book has been designed to teach you the most popular key chord combinations and patterns that you'll see in hundreds of songs. The tunes taught here include: Auld Lang Syne - My Bonnie Lies Over the Ocean - Oh! Susanna - Peg of My Heart - Red River Valley - Tiger Rag - and many more. You can strum the chords for each, or play the easy-to-follow melody.
00001359...$14.99

KEV'S QUICKSTART FINGERSTYLE UKULELE
INCLUDES TAB

by Kevin Rones
Go Beyond Three Chords And A Strum!
This book/CD package is for anyone who want to become better at playing the ukulele.

Newbies: Have fun learning how to play Fingerstyle Ukulele quickly without having to read music! **Ukulele Strummers:** Tired of strumming the same old chords? This book will have you picking in no time! **Indie Artist and Songwriters:** Expand you song writing and performance with Fingerstyle Ukulele. **Guitars players:** If you already play guitar this book is your shortcut into learning Ukulele. Learn arrangements written specifically for Fingerstyle Ukulele: Bach, Blues, Folk, Celtic and more!
000001590...$17.99

UKULELE FOR COWBOYS
INCLUDES TAB

40 of your favorite cowboy songs in chords, standard notation and tab. Includes: Buffalo Gals • Night Herding Song • Doney Gal • Old Chisholm Trail • The Big Corral • Ragtime Cowboy Joe • Colorado Trail • Old Paint • Yellow Rose of Texas • Green Grow the Lilacs • and many more. Also includes a chord chart, historical background on many of the songs, and a short story on the history of the Hawaiian Cowboy.
00000408 ....$14.99

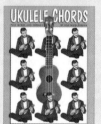

UKULELE SONGBOOK
INCLUDES TAB

compiled by Ron Middlebrook
This terrific collection for beginning to advanced ukulele players features easy arrangements of 50 great songs, in standard notation and tablature. Also teaches popular strum patterns, and how to tune the uke.
00000248...$9.95

UKULELE CHORDS
Plus Intros and Endings

by Ron Middlebrook
This handy chart includes clear, easy-to-see chord fingerings in all keys, plus a bonus section that provides favorite intros and endings in different keys. Also includes information on relative tuning.
00000246 ....$2.95

SONGS OF THE CIVIL WAR FOR UKULELE

by Dick Sheridan
25 tunes of the era that boosted morale, championed causes, pulled on the heartstrings, or gave impetus to battle. Includes: All Quiet Along the Potomac, Aura Lee, Battle Hymn of the Republic, Dixie, The Girl I Left Behind Me, John Brown's Body, When Johnny Comes Marching Home and more - all in standard C tuning, with notation, tablature and accompanying lyrics. The book also includes notes on the songs, historical commentary, and a handy chord chart!
00001588...$14.99

THE LOW G STRING TUNING UKULELE
INCLUDES TAB

by Ron Middlebrook
25 popular songs for the ukulele in standard music notation, tablature and easy chords. To get the most out of this book, you'll want to replace the fourth (high G) string with one of a heavier gauge and tune it an octave lower to get that full, deep sound – a lá Hawaiian uke virtuoso Jesse Kalima – in playing the melodies in this book. The chords can be played with or without the low G sound.
00001534 Book/CD Pack $19.99

CENTERSTREAM®

P.O. Box 17878 - Anaheim Hills, CA 92817
(714) 779-9390   www.centerstream-usa.com